M000305086

The Clever Tykes® Books

Walk-it Willow

Illustrated by Sam Moore

For anyone with a passion

Chapter 1: The Soggy Dog

Willow loved looking after Stomp,

her big shaggy dog. He was very playful and liked to

chase birds on their walks. Her mum and dad

worked a lot and they didn't have time to walk

Stomp, so they were glad that Willow wanted to help.

Sometimes, though, she could be a bit forgetful. She

even forgot that today was Stomp's bath day.

"Willow! You need to give Stomp a bath! He stinks!"

shouted Mum.

"Pee-yoo!" cried Dad. "He smells awful!"

As soon as Stomp heard the word 'bath', he ran

away and hid. Willow tried her best to track him

down – it was always easy to find him because he was so big and hairy. But today, Stomp was doing his best to hide. He did not like baths one bit.

"Stomp. Where are you?" called Willow.

No reply. Where was Stomp?

"Stomp!" called Willow again. Then she had an idea how she could lure him out.

"I have a delicious doggy snack for you. Come and get it!" she shouted loudly.

"Doggy snack?" thought Stomp. "I'd love one of those."

He crawled out from the bushes in the garden and raced back inside to Willow. Time for a tasty snack!

Stomp looked at Willow. She was holding something in her hand. It didn't look like a doggy snack - it looked like a bottle. Uh oh! It was a bottle of doggy shampoo.

"Ha ha, I tricked you!" cheered Willow, grabbing Stomp's collar and leading him to his bath. Stomp sulked all the way there, grumpy there was no tasty snack, just a horrible bath.

Willow managed to steer smelly Stomp into the bath and poured water over him. He stood there very forlorn indeed – he hated every drop that fell on his fluffy head.

He looked around for an escape route. Should he leap through the window? Should he flush himself down the toilet and escape through the sewers?

Suddenly Stomp spotted a way out – silly Willow forgot to close the bathroom door!

He quickly leapt out of the bathtub and dashed out of the bathroom.

"OH NO. NOT AGAIN!" cried Willow in despair.

Stomp charged down the stairs, his wet fur dripping all over the carpet. Towel in hand, Willow ran after him, desperate to dry the soggy dog.

"ARGH!" screamed Willow's mum from the kitchen. "He's still wet! Willow! You need to dry him as well!"

"Sorry, Mum! He ran away again!" shouted Willow, speeding past.

Stomp made his way towards the garden. He wanted to jump into the big pile of leaves he'd found earlier.

Willow ran as fast as she could, leapt high into the air and landed right in front of Stomp. He screeched to a halt, then turned to run away again...

"You're not going to get away from me this time, you wet mutt!"

Willow pulled the towel out wide and launched herself towards her pet. Before he knew it, he was captured in the towel. "Naughty Stomp! You can't escape now! I need to dry you."

Stomp gave a small but happy bark. He didn't mean to be naughty, he just really wanted to jump into the leaves.

Willow quickly dried the soggy dog before he tried to escape again. As soon as he was drier, they ran back inside.

Mum set down a bowl of meaty chunks for Stomp and handed Willow a glass of water.

"Thank you for looking after Stomp," she said. "But next time, please make sure you close the bathroom door. You know that all he wants to do is run and play."

Willow nodded, feeling guilty for being forgetful.

"Sorry Mum. I promise to be more responsible next time."

Just as she spoke, there was a sudden noise.

KNOCK KNOCK!

Chapter 2: A visitor at the door

Stomp darted from his bowl, straight to the front door, barking loudly. "Stranger! Stranger!" he shouted. But the family didn't understand dog-speak.

"Shush, Stomp. Get back to the kitchen. Now who could that be?" asked Willow's dad suspiciously. They weren't expecting any visitors today.

As he answered the door, a familiar smell of overpowering perfume crept into the house. It was Miss Snippet from down the road at number 10.

Stomp yelped and ran away. His sensitive doggy nose could not cope with the super-flowery smell of Miss Snippet's perfume. Yuck!

Miss Snippet wore lots of make-up and brightly coloured clothes. Willow thought it made her look a bit like a clown but she did her best not to giggle.

"Oh, hello there, Miss Snippet," said Willow's dad. "Is everything okay?" (She only ever visited their house to complain about noise or a bush that was growing too big.)

"Hello!" cried Miss Snippet in her shrill voice, her lipstick-stained teeth making everyone shudder in terror. "I've come to ask a favour, dearie. Could I speak to your sweet daughter?"

"Y-yes, of course," said Willow's dad, holding his breath. He spluttered at the smell of perfume that oozed from Miss Snippet.

"Hello, my dear," said Miss Snippet shaking Willow's hand firmly. Her varnished nails were long and sharp like bird claws.

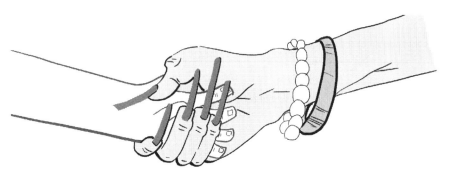

"I've seen you walking that big dog of yours. You seem to know how to keep him under control, so I think I can trust you!" Willow was confused and a little surprised that Miss Snippet had noticed her walking Stomp.

"Trust me to do what?" she asked politely.

"My sweet Mr Snuggles is looking a little too big these days. He's been eating too many snacks from somewhere," said Miss Snippet.

Willow knew that Miss Snippet liked to feed scraps and snacks to her dog. That was why he was getting so big.

"It's not my fault, of course, but I think he needs more walks," Miss Snippet said. "Could you do that for me?"

Willow looked at her parents who both nodded. "It would be a great way to show how responsible you are," agreed her mum.

"And I'll give you some money for helping me. It will be my way of saying 'thank you'," continued Miss Snippet.

Willow smiled and thanked Miss Snippet. She was excited that she had the chance to walk another dog. Dogs were Willow's favourite animals.

"Maybe I could start a dog-walking service for all of the neighbours," thought Willow.

*

Later that week, after a busy day at school, Willow and her friend Rupa were enjoying a slow stroll home. Willow told Rupa all about Miss Snippet's visit. Rupa was amazed.

"That's brilliant Willow! I know how much you like walking Stomp. It will be great to walk ANOTHER dog."

"I know! I can't wait to get started!" said Willow."

"When are you taking Mr Snuggles for his first walk?" asked her friend.

"Oh, it's not until Thursday," said Willow.

"But it's Thursday today!" replied Rupa. They both stopped walking.

Willow's eyes widened. "Oh no, not AGAIN!" Forgetful Willow began running home, as fast as her legs could go.

She had only a few minutes to get changed, collect Stomp and run to Miss Snippet's house! She ran into the house and dashed up the stairs to her room. Would she make it to Miss Snippet's house on time?

Chapter 3: The First Walk

Willow changed at lightning speeds, raced out of her room and down the stairs into the kitchen to fetch Stomp.

She glanced at her watch.

Tick-tick-tick.

Time was running out. Willow couldn't be late on her first day.

Willow and Stomp charged out of the house and towards number 10. They leapt over Miss Snippet's fence and up to the front door. Willow reached out her hand and quickly pressed the doorbell.

TRA-LA-DING TRA-LA-DING-DING-DONG

Miss Snippet appeared at the door. "Oh hello, deary. Glad you could make it! Here he is: my lovely, adorable, super, fluffy, gorgeous Mr Snuggles."

There, at Miss Snippet's feet was a pink poodle – he looked as silly as his owner! With his sparkly sequin collar and leopard-print dog coat, Willow felt a bit sorry for him.

After seeing that his new friend was dressed rather strangely, Stomp tried to hide behind Willow. He wasn't sure he wanted other dogs to see him with Mr Snuggles.

Miss Snippet gave Willow the lead for Mr Snuggles – it was bright pink! Stomp shook his head in disgust.

"Okay dogs! Let's go!" said Willow cheerily, waving goodbye to Miss Snippet.

They were only a little way down the road when Willow felt a tug on Mr Snuggles' lead. It was clear Mr Snuggles did not like walks. He tried with all his might to turn back home, tugging hard on the lead and pulling back towards number 10.

"Come on, Mr Snuggles, stop being naughty! This walk is good for you. It will make you a healthy dog."

Mr Snuggles flopped onto the floor. He refused to walk any more.

"It looks like all those snacks have made you into a very lazy dog indeed," said Willow.

As Willow worked out how she could get Mr Snuggles to walk, a bird landed on a nearby car. Stomp fixed his eyes on it, watching its every move.

"Tweet!"

Willow spotted the bird. Stomp stared at it, not even blinking. Willow knew exactly what would happen next.

"Uh-oh! You'll need to start moving soon, Mr Snuggles. We need to ru-"

But before she could finish speaking, Stomp barked loudly. The startled bird jumped and flew down the street. Stomp bolted after it...

...taking Willow and Mr Snuggles with him!

"YARGH! STOMP! STOOOOP!" shouted Willow.

The bird flew high up into the air.

"Come back here, bird!" barked Stomp, but it was too late. The bird was high up in the sky.

Stomp stopped running. Willow's legs felt like jelly but when she peered around to look at Mr Snuggles, she saw him wagging his tail happily!

"See!" said Willow, patting the pink poodle, "walks aren't so bad after all!"

After that, Mr Snuggles stopped being naughty and began to enjoy his walk.

Stomp and Mr Snuggles soon became really good dog-friends. They raced each other and jumped together; they chased birds and barked at the scary cars.

And when they reached Radish Park, the dogs barked at the ducks by the lake and rolled in piles of leaves and mud.

Afterward, they walked by the playground and chased toy helicopters and toy cars.

It would have been really difficult to take Mr Snuggles for a walk if he didn't want to go anywhere. Luckily, he was having a great time – in fact, they all were.

In all the excitement, Willow lost track of time. She looked at her watch – it was already getting late and she needed to do her science homework and have dinner.

"That's enough adventures for today! Let's go home!" she sighed. As they headed home, Willow saw a familiar face. It was Mr Moore!

Chapter 4: Mr Moore

Mr Moore was a
friend of Willow's
parents. He always
dressed smartly and
he was a very busy
man.

He was walking his
dog, Pepper, a tall dog who moved calmly. She was
very well-behaved and didn't bark at anything. She
definitely didn't roll around in mud!

"Hello, Mr Moore!" smiled Willow.

"Hello, Willow. Stomp, you've grown to be a very big dog indeed!" said Mr Moore.

Stomp recognised Mr Moore and jumped up to greet him, wagging his tail and barking happily.

"And who might your new friend be?" asked Mr Moore, looking at the pink poodle.

"This is Mr Snuggles," explained Willow. "Miss Snippet asked me to walk him and she is giving me some money to help her out. I might offer a dog-walking service for all of my neighbours."

Mr Moore smiled. "An excellent idea!" he exclaimed. "That would be a really valuable service."

Stomp and Mr Snuggles wanted to say hello to Pepper so they sniffed her clean fur but she didn't

want to be near the muddy, scruffy dogs. She crept behind her owner and turned her head away in disgust.

"Everyone needs something," continued Mr Moore. "If you need food, you go to a shop to buy it. If you need electricity for your house, you pay the power company to provide it. Some people need their dogs walking and that's where you come in!"

Willow suddenly understood the value in a dog-walking service. She enjoyed doing it and people like Miss Snippet needed her help. Willow knew she could find more dogs to walk.

Mr Moore gave some more good advice to Willow. "Save some of the money that people give you for walking their dogs. Use it to pay for spare leads or to buy small bags! You can't avoid stinky dog mess but you must always clean it up!"

"Thank you for the advice Mr Moore!" said Willow. He was always very helpful whenever he came to visit the family.

"It's quite alright," grinned Mr Moore. "Would you like to walk Pepper too? I usually have lots of meetings in the week, so it would help me out."

Willow was just about to answer, when a horrid stench filled the air. Mr Moore's face turned bright red and Willow held her breath as best as she could. It seemed Mr Moore was right when he said stinky dog mess couldn't be avoided: Mr Snuggles had pooped!

The smell was disgusting!

Bleurgh! What was Miss Snippet feeding him? Her perfume? Rotten eggs? A sandwich filled with smelly socks?

Mr Moore, held his breath as he handed a small plastic bag to Willow.

"I'll... call... mmph... your...parents... later... to talk about... walking... Pepper!"

He walked off as fast as he could and Pepper happily followed him. Even Stomp moved away from his stinky pink doggy-friend. Yuck!

Willow held her nose feeling happy that she had a new dog to walk but unhappy that Mr Snuggles had made a mess. Now she had to clean it up. Pee-yoo!

Chapter 5: How to get more dogs

After returning Mr Snuggles to Miss Snippet and bringing Stomp home, Willow wondered how she could find more dogs to walk.

"I know! I'll wear something when I walk dogs. Other people will be able to see that I provide a dog-walking service."

Willow invited her friend Rupa round to her house. Rupa was very creative at school and Willow knew

she would come up with some interesting ideas.

"We should try putting a sign on a hat!" suggested Rupa.

But Willow couldn't stand up straight because it was too heavy for her head!

"We should make a giant sandwich-board sign!" suggested Rupa.

But Willow couldn't walk properly because it was too big for her arms and legs!

"Erm.... We could try..." Rupa was running out of ideas.

"Here! Try this!" Willow's mum shouted out of nowhere.

Something flew through the air, straight towards Willow. Stomp leapt and grabbed it with his teeth!

"Oops! Sorry sweetie," said her Mum, as Stomp politely gave the bundle to Willow. She unrolled it to reveal a t-shirt. It looked amazing!

Willow and Rupa were so busy thinking of crazy hats and signs that they forgot to try a simple idea like a t-shirt.

"Look" said her mum.

"I've created an email address for you. When you wear this, people can see it. They can email you if they want you to walk their dog!"

"Wow!" said Rupa to Willow. "Your Mum is the best!"

Willow nodded. "Thank you, Mum," she beamed.

*

Willow made sure that she wore the t-shirt every time she took Stomp, Mr Snuggles or Pepper for a walk. Lots of people noticed it and asked Willow about her dog-walking service.

"Do you have a lot of experience walking dogs?" asked a short man with a French bulldog.

Willow spoke very politely: "Yes of course, sir. I already walk two neighbours' dogs, and my own. I make sure they enjoy their walks and that they walk as much as they need to."

"Do you clean up their mess?" asked a young woman.

"Of course, madam!" said Willow. "I am in charge of looking after the dogs and clearing any mess they make."

"How do I contact you? I might ask you to walk my dog, too!" asked one gentleman.

"Here's my email address," replied Willow, pointing to her t-shirt. "Send me a message and my mum and I will get back to you!"

Willow and her mum loved to check the emails every day. Sometimes there would be a new message from someone who wanted Willow to walk their dog!

Willow made sure she replied to every email. She didn't want to ignore anybody who could be a future customer.

She arranged the date and time for

when she would walk each new dog. In just a few weeks, Willow had lots of dogs to walk.

Mr Bing, who lived near Radish Park, had a Dalmatian called Boing. Boing found everything exciting and jumped up at new people to say 'hello'.

Miss Berry had a small terrier called Hollie, who liked hiding under things. Miss Berry couldn't see very well in her old age, so it often took a long time for her to find Hollie.

Mr and Mrs Chimney had a dog called Smokey. Even though Smokey was a very big dog, he was scared by little things. A leaf! Yikes!

Willow couldn't wait to take the new dogs for their walks.

Chapter 6: Smokey, Hollie and Boing

Willow took each of the new dogs for a first walk on
their own to see how easy or difficult it would be to

look after them.

On the first day, Willow
took Boing the Dalmatian.
Mr Bing travelled lots so
he often needed someone
to walk his dog.

Boing was very friendly.
Whenever people walked

by he would jump and bark!

WOOF!

But the people didn't understand dog-speak; they thought Boing was barking in a mean way. Willow found herself having to say sorry an awful lot.

"Sorry sir! He's just saying hello! Sorry, madam! He likes meeting new people!"

"Hmm," thought Willow. "These walks will be good for calming you down. You'll get bored of saying hello to every single person you meet!"

On the second day, Willow took Smokey for his first walk. Smokey was very different from Boing. He ran up the stairs when Willow went to Mr and Mrs Chimney's house to collect him and yelped whenever he saw a bee or butterfly. He cowered as cars

drove past.

These walks will be good for making you a bit braver," thought Willow.

On the third day, Willow took Hollie the terrier for her walk.

"I have no idea where she is," laughed Miss Berry. "I can't find her anywhere!" Willow peered into the hallway and saw Hollie hiding behind the coat-stand.

"There she is!" laughed Willow.

Hollie was even more troublesome on the walk. She dived under bushes and scurried under parked cars. She was like a mouse, running away and hiding all the time! It was difficult to walk when Hollie kept disappearing.

"No more hiding for you, Hollie," declared Willow. "These walks will be good for keeping you in the great outdoors."

Willow couldn't wait to take all these new dogs for more walks and help them become better behaved. She was sure their owners would be very pleased.

Willow told Rupa all about the adventures she'd had when she took the new dogs for their first walks.

"Hollie is so adorable, she loves hiding! Oh, and Smokey is a big softie! Boing is really friendly too!" she enthused.

"It's great your dog-walking service is doing so well. You are already meeting and walking so many new dogs!" smiled Rupa.

"Yes," replied Willow. "I'm starting to make some money, too. But I make sure that I use it to buy more dog mess bags. I save the rest!"

Rupa was impressed, "I wish I'd have thought of something like that!"

That evening, Willow did her chores and homework. It had been a busy day with lots to do and she was looking forward to a long, relaxing walk with Stomp.

Before they set off, Willow logged onto her emails to see when she was walking the other dogs. Willow saw that she was booked to walk Boing the following day. She'd also agreed to take Smokey.

"Hmm, I can manage these two and Stomp," she thought.

But as Willow continued to look through her emails, she realised to her horror that she'd agreed to walk all the dogs the next day at the same time!

She realised with a sinking feeling that she hadn't checked her timetable when she booked the dogs in for their walks.

Willow panicked. How would she walk SIX DOGS at the SAME TIME? Pepper didn't like Stomp and Mr Snuggles; Smokey was too scared of other dogs; and it would be difficult to stop Boing from jumping and Hollie from hiding.

She checked all her emails to see if she had made a mistake. No, she wasn't imagining things. She'd agreed to walk all the dogs the following day at the same time. Willow felt so foolish – why had she not checked before?

"I don't want to upset my customers," thought Willow. "I will have to take ALL the dogs for their walk, even if it will be VERY difficult!"

Gulp

Willow couldn't sleep that night. All she could think about was walking six dogs.

Even her dreams made her worry: in them, she held a huge lead that was attached to six giant dogs! No matter how loudly she shouted, they just wouldn't listen to her. They jumped onto houses and their barks were deafening. Oh no! Giant-sized Mr Snuggles was about to make a giant-sized poop!

Willow woke up in a cold sweat. Stomp. Mr Snuggles. Pepper. Hollie. Smokey. Boing: all six dogs were going for their walk at the same time!

Chapter 7: Too many dogs

The next day, Willow was still very nervous and her parents could tell she was worried about something.

"Is everything OK, Willow?" asked her concerned dad.

"Erm. Yes, Dad. Everything's fine," fibbed Willow.

She didn't want her parents to know that she had accidentally arranged to walk all the dogs at once. If Willow could walk the six dogs without any problems, it would show her mum and dad that she was responsible.

Willow suddenly felt very positive: "I can do it!" she thought.

That evening, as the sky grew cloudy and grey, Willow set out to walk the dogs. She made sure she told her mum and dad where she was going.

"I'll be home in a little while," said Willow. "I'm just taking Stomp and a few others for their walks!"

"Make sure you are back in time for dinner," called back her mum from the living room.

She collected Stomp and then went to number 10 to collect Mr Snuggles.

"Be careful tonight, deary," advised Miss Snippet, who was putting on even more lipstick. "It looks like rain is on the way!"

Willow peered up and saw dark gloomy clouds in the distance – it was going to be difficult enough

walking six dogs, but six WET dogs in the rain?! It
didn't bear thinking about.

Willow started to walk more quickly because she
worried about the approaching rain, but Mr
Snuggles struggled to keep up. She stopped to

collect Hollie, Smokey and Boing and tried her best to look confident and happy.

"My, my, you are walking a lot of dogs tonight, Willow!" said Mr Bing, looking at the four dogs beside Willow. "Are you sure you can manage so many?"

"Of course!" said Willow. She held Stomp and Smokey's leads in one hand. In her other hand she held the leads of Mr Snuggles and Hollie.

Next, Boing joined the gang. "So far, so good!" thought Willow.

The last house to visit was Mr Moore's, where she would collect Pepper. As he opened the door, Mr Moore peered down at the large group of dogs

surrounding Willow.

"Wow, five already! That's a lot of dogs," said Mr
Moore.

Willow didn't want Mr Moore to worry. She
remembered something she had read in a book at
school. "It's quite all right, Mr Moore. It's good for
the dogs! I learned that they like being in groups.
Having this many dogs together at the same time

will make them more friendly!"

Mr Moore nodded and handed over Pepper's lead. "That sounds good to me! You seem to know what you're doing. Hopefully you won't all get too wet!"

The dark clouds crept closer.

"Thank you," said Willow as she left. This was it! She had six dogs! All she needed to do was take them for a walk. What could go wrong?

Chapter 8: Disaster

Willow and the dogs walked
down the road to Radish Park.
All six were surprisingly calm
and well behaved. They didn't try to run, jump or
hide.

"This will be easy! I didn't need to worry!" thought
Willow happily.

But then the sky grew darker and a raindrop fell.
Then another raindrop and another raindrop. Then
it poured down! The rain was so heavy!

"Oh no!" shrieked Willow. "We need to find
somewhere to shelter!"

They were all soaked
before they could find
cover and the dogs all
shook their fur, which
made Willow even
wetter.

The rain continued to pour down heavily as they
made their way to the park. Willow looked for some
trees to hide under but it was becoming increasingly
difficult to handle the dogs. They didn't like this wet
weather one bit!

Hollie started diving under
parked cars and to avoid the
rain, while Smokey yelped at
the scary puddles.

Boing jumped up and down as
people hurried past with their umbrellas and

Mr Snuggles cowered by Willow as he didn't want to get his pretty pink fur all wet.

Pepper kept pulling away from the other dogs because they were stinky and wet and although Stomp wanted to help Willow, there was nothing he could do. This gentle walk had turned into a disaster!

"Please, dogs!" begged Willow. "Please walk nicely. There are six of you and only one of me! You're making it very difficult!" But, of course, the dogs didn't understand human-speak so they continued to jump, hide, chase, cower, bark and pull at their leads. Stomp barked at them all but the other dogs didn't listen to him.

Willow held the leads as tightly as she could and walked down the road as carefully as possible. Suddenly, the leads started to feel tighter in her hands. Were the dogs trying to run away?

She looked at her hands and then her eyes moved down towards the dogs. With all the jumping and

54

hiding and moving, the leads had become jumbled up.

"Oh dear. This can't get any worse!" thought Willow, as she carefully moved the leads from one hand to the other as she attempted to untangle them.

It was very complicated! Hollie had to loop over Stomp and Mr Snuggles needed to move in between Smokey and Boing. Pepper had to move closer so that the other leads could move more freely.

Just as Willow passed Pepper's lead from one hand to the other, Pepper pulled really hard and broke free!

"Pepper! No!" Pepper was loose!

"Please stay there!" begged Willow as she leaned over to grab the handle of Pepper's lead.

But she wasn't quick enough – Pepper wanted to get out of the horrid rain, so she darted out of the park! Pepper's lead trailed along the ground and was sliding away from her like a snake.

It was too late.

Stomp barked loudly, demanding that Pepper comes back to the group.

"PEPPER!" shouted Willow.

It was no use. Pepper was gone!

Chapter 9: Don't Panic

Willow knew she had to stay calm and think how she was going to find Pepper.

Willow walked out of the park and headed down the road that Pepper had run into. She had a difficult decision to make because she still had the other five

dogs with her.

"I could look for Pepper with these dogs with me, even though they're really wet and tired," she

thought. Mr Snuggles was already lying on the wet ground, feeling very weary.

She needed to put the dogs somewhere – she knew she couldn't take them with her.

"I could tie the leads to a lamp-post and then look for Pepper!" said Willow but immediately decided that was a bad idea. "No! I can't do that. Someone could take them or they could all break free!"

If she lost six dogs all at once she would never be trusted to walk dogs again!

"I'll take these dogs back to their owners, then I can look for

Pepper," Willow decided.

Nervously, Willow took each dog back to its home. Boing was happy to see Mr Bing again. He'd made lots of friends that day but he was back with his favourite person!

Hollie ran into Miss Berry's house and hid beneath the lovely warm radiator.

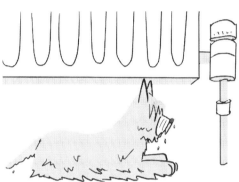

Smokey leapt up to Mrs Chimney, glad to be home and away from the scary puddles!

Mr Snuggles crawled into the hallway of Miss Snippet's house and started snoozing on the stairs.

"That walk took a little longer tonight," said Miss Snippet. "Did this awful weather cause any problems?"

Willow did her very best to hide her worry about Pepper. "Just a few wet dogs today, Miss Snippet."

"Not to worry," continued Miss Snippet, "Mr Snuggles will sleep very well tonight after so much exercise."

Lastly, Willow took Stomp back home. If she could do it without her parents seeing her, she could go back outside to find Pepper and still be home in time for dinner. They would never know that she had lost Mr Moore's dog!

Willow carefully opened the front door and saw light coming from the living room – her mum and dad were watching television.

"Shhh!" she whispered to Stomp as they crept

upstairs. They tiptoed, avoiding the creaky

floorboards, and finally reached her bedroom.

Willow threw some spare blankets in a corner. "Lie

down here, Stomp. Please don't make any noise! If

Mum and Dad know that I'm outside looking for

Pepper they'll be very cross with me."

Stomp listened and rolled his wet fur on

the cosy blankets before falling to sleep.

Willow gently closed her bedroom door

and quietly crept down the stairs towards the front door. She reached out to turn the door handle silently...

"We didn't hear you come in!"

It was Willow's dad – his voice made her jump.

She gulped and tried to think of a response.

"Erm... I... erm... well..." There were wet paw prints all the way up the stairs. It was obvious that she had brought Stomp back home.

"Is everything alright?" he asked. Willow couldn't keep it a secret anymore. She needed to be honest.

"I lost Mr Moore's dog, Pepper. I'm so sorry, Dad. I needed to take all the dogs at once. It started to rain and-" Willow began to cry.

"Calm down, Willow. Are all the other dogs back with their owners?" asked her dad.

"Y-yes" said Willow, wiping the tears from her eyes.

"That was very sensible of you. Now we can sort out this problem. We'll speak with Mr Moore. It's too dark and wet to look for Pepper now," he said.

Willow was very upset. Everything had gone so terribly wrong and she knew Mr Moore would never forgive her. She would never be allowed to walk dogs again.

Chapter 10: Bad news for Mr Moore

Dad knocked on Mr Moore's door. Willow stood timidly next to him, afraid of what Mr Moore would say.

She stared at the floor as Mr Moore opened the door. Her legs felt shaky and she tried her best not to cry.

"Mr Moore. I– I'm afraid I have some bad news. You see... it all happened so fast. I was walking too many dogs. Then it started to rain. I'm sorry! I'm sorry Mr Moore, but Pepper ran away!" Willow felt terrible about what happened.

Mr Moore looked very stern and said: "Willow, I think you should both come in." Willow was certain she saw him smile as he turned.

Willow and her dad stepped into Mr Moore's house.

Mr Moore suddenly gave two sharp whistles.

Dad and Willow looked at each other. Why was Mr Moore whistling?

Willow couldn't believe it: Pepper was here! She'd

made it back home!

"I thought she'd gone forever," said a relieved Willow, bending down to stroke Pepper.

"Pepper is very clever," said Mr Moore. "She always knows the way home wherever she goes." Willow beamed widely, happy to see Pepper safe and sound!

"I'm sorry that I let her go, Mr Moore, I didn't mean to," said Willow.

"Everyone makes mistakes, Willow, and accidents happen," said Mr Moore. "Why did you try to handle so many dogs all at once?"

"I forgot to check my emails properly," admitted Willow, "then I didn't want to let anyone down."

Mr Moore understood.

"If you run any type of business, you need to manage your time well," he advised her in a kind voice.

"If you take on too much yourself, things can go wrong. Keep a proper diary and make sure each customer receives an excellent service."

Willow agreed. She knew she was forgetful. "I will be more careful! I'll keep checking my timetable for when each dog needs to be walked, and make sure not to book too many on the same day."

"If you have lots of dogs to walk, it means lots of people want to use your service," continued Mr Moore.

"You'll need other people to help you to walk the dogs. Is there anyone you could ask? If you give them some of the money that you make, I'm sure they'll be happy to help!"

Willow knew *exactly* who could help her!

"That advice from Mr Moore will help you to avoid any more disasters," Willow's dad told her, nodding towards his friend.

"He's always been successful in business, providing services for people. He has whole teams that help him now!"

"I know you didn't mean to lose Pepper, so here's the

money I owe you," said Mr Moore, handing an envelope to Willow. "Remember, if you need help, don't be afraid to ask for it."

Now that they knew Pepper was safe, Willow and her dad turned to leave for home. Dinner was getting cold but Willow had something on her mind and wanted to ask Mr Moore one more question.

"Did you ever make mistakes, Mr Moore?"

Mr Moore nodded and chuckled. "Yes of course, too many to mention! It's okay to make mistakes but it's important to learn from them."

"Thank you, Mr Moore!" said Willow politely as she

and Dad left. "I've learned a lot from what happened today. I promise it will never ever happen again!"

Chapter 11: A helping hand

Willow's mum and dad were very proud of how she handled the problem.

She'd been honest with Mr Moore and had taken responsibility for losing Pepper. Most importantly, she'd learned from her mistakes.

Since it had happened, Willow's mum and dad often tested her to see if she knew when each dog needed to be taken for a walk. After all, she could still be a bit forgetful.

"When do you need to walk Boing?" asked her mum.

"Thursday and then Tuesday!"

"When do you need to walk Pepper?" asked her dad.

"Monday, Thursday and Sunday!"

Willow quickly became much better at organising the walks and by following Mr Moore's advice, she didn't walk too many dogs at once and no more tangled leads. Thankfully, no more dogs ran away from her!

But what made the walks even more fun was that she now had help from her friend Rupa!

Willow couldn't wait to meet more new people and their dogs. Every new email she received filled her with excitement - which breed of dog would she be asked to walk next?

Willow was very glad she decided to run her own dog-walking service! And the busy people in her neighbourhood were thrilled they had someone they could rely on to do a good service.

THE END

Walk-it Willow is the first in the series of the Clever Tykes books. We really hope you enjoyed reading it and be sure to check out the other titles in the series.

If you'd like to learn more about the Clever Tykes books visit www.CleverTykes.com - we'd love to hear from you!

You can even send an email to Willow and tell her what you think of her story: willow@clevertykes.com

You'll find us on Facebook and follow Clever Tykes on Twitter @CleverTykes

Written by Jason, Ben and Jodie.

Made in United States
Orlando, FL
13 September 2022